FRIMAIRE

FRIMAIRE

POETRY BY MARK LAMOUREUX

CONTENTS

Foreword: This Machine Kills Fascists

& in the bubble of
the still eye I call
on the ghosts of my heroes

wherever they may
rest & they come
out of the sun as a moth-

winged deva, a milky
shadow above
the galled land;

it draws a bead
on a fascist & lets go
three bolts of the pure light

of the unowned
moon & they strike
deep in the barrel

of the empty chest & still
the heart that is not a heart
but a gibbering

foul mouth; my love
sets upon them like
a feral dog, manic

with wan blood,
patinaed by the grey
dust of their empty

buildings. My love
is the half-moon scythe,
the storms at sea;

it will pluck out their angry eyes,
crush their empty heads
like the fat grapes

of maenads; it will drink
long & grow awful
& strong in the face of god,

1

though there is no god.
I am
the priest of nightmares;

I spit
on their hungry flames
& extinguish. My love

is the brazen tornado,
my love is a plague
of locusts, a murrain,

the burning fields,
the withering scream
of the void.

MISERICORDATE

My heart   of chrome
reflects   sensation;
bleeds   fuel rods
in the center   of the silver
machine,   a corkscrew
       in the anvil
       of the night.

My heart of crystal
looks   into the
future & the past
like the wounded eye
of my love, the lashes that squeeze
hourglass sand to diamonds
in the barrel of the chest.

My heart of coral
rips the feet   of my love
to shreds,   down
the Bimini   Road
with a necklace of jet
wings.   The fists
of barnacles knock
on the door of the skull.

My heart of water
floats   the votives,
blasts   the mausoleum
with silver   refrains.

My heart of air
is a ghost   in the rain,
stippled & obliterated,
fuel   for songs
choked with leaves, pecks
at the unmarked grave
like a blackbird in the green
storm.

My heart of onion
paper   brings
my love to tears,
but it's nothing

        I did
        today.

My heart of glass
is a pain in the ass,
kills   starlings,
fogs up   under its
mask,   cries
with its mouth, does nothing
with its eyes.

My heart of stone,
ballast   for the black
ship   on the sea
of blood; beating
in the breast   bone
yard   down
where the dead men go, where
the ghosts climb up
the throat like a song.

My heart of fire
consumes   the pyre
of   my brittle bones
burns   on the waves
of my resting   mind.

My heart of flesh
is torn   like a carnival
ticket   to ride
the Matterhorn, its spokes
of light light   the cavern
of the solar   plexus, spin
like the quick hands
of the life   clock
ticking inside

My heart of hearts
on all the cards;   the
misericorde   in
my ear   points
the way home.   The
king who rains   & rains
on either side,   neither up
nor down,   foretells
nothing & to nothing I shall
return when

My heart   of clockwork
grinds   the chaff
to the   staff
of the hermit   who hides
in the shell   of the man,
          the mother   of pearl
is the daughter   of stardust
of the diamonds   in the mouths
          of the dead.

My heart   of darkness
will quell   your burns,
points the way
from the Bauhaus smile
                              of the gnomon.

My heart   of earth
buries   its dead
who shall   not rise
but   burn
like   Venus
in the dawn.

My heart   in a jar
on a shelf   on the wall,
wet   specimen
in a bath   of tears;
the spark
          traverses the alembic
          to where words
          are collected & worlds.

BLAST BEAT

It is the sound
        of breaking backs,
the crackle of ruin—
        the castle opens its eyes,
quiet grey god
        who rides the dispossessed.
The devil I know,
        calloused front of the hand
who labors for nothing—
        fruit without taste or texture.
Millennial recidivist,
        binary amnesia
in a web of locked-down signals.

Litany of passwords;
        the workforce leaks data.
Weariness of the record,
        the dark
stenographer's
        eyes that reach
from the cenotaph.
        Creased palm
that rocks
        the bier of junk
& gewgaws of code,
        code of ethics
misplaced in the boilerplate.
        The sacrosanct
documents the contract,
        social net
work, worth, a slick web
        of the quiet
orb-weaver, just a
        spinning sphere
in space falling
        slowly into the sun.

As Dark As Day

The text of

an endless announcement

Ladies & gentlemen

expect service interruptions

Rivulets of the future

& the past running

out the mad god's ears

the streams of his tears

the lives of others

the ones in stories

or the ones on the train

Your mouth eclipsed

by the signal flare

as along the horizon

crowning stately towers

the code is spread

across the coils

of the people, an antigen

for songs

I am

among

you not

of

you

MEKOCHE

Beyond
the nape
of the mountain,
where water is money:

biochemical
ritual in the cone of skin
giving old true names
to these exertions:

the fluid of the air

this reagent

hollows bones for flight

O pinion donor

uncoiling in the curlicue

of your human mind.

Quills horns teeth;
the marzipan pads of feet;
the star cuts a tail-groove in the sage;
the limbs swing, a sweaty
curtain that spills

onto the cold foam: advances
& retreats in crustacean steps.

The lid of a carapace,
a cocoon, seals overhead;
the gold placental light,

a pure note that smites
the human wrack
in the animal town of the head.

FOOLSCAP

See I'm still
nothing; the world
smells like strawberry ice-cream,
celestial body
language. A recidivist
in the new
math, a lock groove
spaces out in the personal
space of your wasted
olden days. A stick
of candy that's just
braided sugar, chartreuse & turquoise,
slick under the tongue, sticky
in the rain. How it rains
is how it rains, brown
or silver on the day you began,
the day you got licked.
It's just negative
capability, the sugar made plastic
by seawater, slurping in the grove
under a little bridge,
a paperback on the water,
dancing like you, the woman
on the cover, going under.
The words will bleed
away, the motives, the herrings
made red & pungent by paprika;
the first person
was ever so lonely, the second was
me, the second
between inhalation & exhalation
the mystery of the waveform,
the ripples of the grooves the microscopic mountains where sound is born.

LULLABY

O you bloom
of my internal violence;
each day's a cake
of the wish to die
& the wish to live
forever in the space
of some brazen
indiscretion. The gong
of the sun wobbles over
the steady ground that is
shook by legs. Taking
a swipe at the curb
like a feral kitten
might. All this fancy footwork
just to get home;
all this long night
just to get some sleep.

SONG FOR BETH HARMON WHO DOESN'T EXIST

For when you are orphan-feral in the eye
of your mind.

For when you dance to the music of the blood
in the ears.

For when you wear the habit
of the morning star.

For when the ice melts
on its own.

For the calling
that is like a hole in the earth.

For all of the wide, tilting earth
as it glitters below.

For every lost thing found
in the cradle of a street.

For barmen & angels
& angles of approach.

For the fallen king,
the queen who rules.

For the insouciance
that burns.

For when god comes
in a flash of silver.

For the endless night;
for the morning after.

For the impossibility
of problems.

For the problem
of consciousness.

For money.

For keeps.

For the last time,
forever & ever

amen.

BLAST BEAT
for Chris McCreary

Underneath the triple-headed skeletal swan
                                 song, chaotic
                neutralized, guitar
floor teeming spasmodic
        motion of kids
& their stages, shoals of hands,
                    a sneaker
breaches, young punks
               submerged in the human
                  breakers—
as much as it hurts, on the periphery;
the balm of a forward bend for the old bones, old boy
heaped up with time.
        The helping hands of the pit are not for you;
you can only gaze in at them:
        another zone,
endurance, plentitude, which is nothing, ultimately.
        Green age being a ship of nothing, hold full up
with other peoples' problems, ballast for the gale-rocked crew,
        sailing expertly for the edge of the known world,
which sure as shit exists,
        prow down over the edge in a log ride stomach-drop,
arms in the air trusting some camera eye to burn onto staid stone tablets
        what you were, what you are
                    in the eternity
        of intention. Childish things
                imbued
        with the life that is the deathless mind
        of matter:
        transubstantiation
of the lead hero, leading
        the party out of darkness
into darkness, the sun being
        a trick of the eye,
              an awful pedantic god
who desiccates the flesh;
the brain lives in the cave
              of the skull, untouched
        by the light of day, the last thing
that moves, interpolating motion,
        the feed of the ears, which ring
with the gone sounds, still lingering,

13

still on fire
with the same songs
as the pit kids,
who are you
                    in intervals, a Doppler wave
that bends away
from the stationary observer
around whom the earth tilts &
            dips the sun in the drink,
an ordinary orange
            full of ordinary days that unravel
like the string of a kite.

THE HELM OF SORROW

Wraiths of quicksilver
rain billowed across the fissure
between worlds as the Exorcist

told his tale to the Mendicant
until the Skullcrusher raspberry
colored dawn

where *Papa will be all alone*
with unclean singing, the purple
tyrannosaur heading

for the exhumed playground.
There's a pandemic
in Tanelorn & those who travel

by night are on their own.
The keep is a cold & lonely place,
but listen carefully because the options have changed

as the magic lasso of the tape
flaps in an unoccupied flat
& the roly polies roll in the shadow

of the ankh.

BARDO

Steel grey on navy blue
        gloaming lichen   nigori cumuli
10 toasts
        throw your hat in
        capillary action
of the sky the jewel box spider
        of a big jet going
        autobiographers of clouds
bodhisattvas & onis
        dapper in the drinking
places unsheath the water-
        knife in the trenchant
dirty townships   On a night like this
        someone is dropping
beats in 1989
        The many flowering bushes
of hell   The blue devils
        crazed from it
            gunpowder & marigold smells
one long mirror
        in the river replete with licks
of flame   billowing coals
        black light
        crushed velvet
        to clean the blade
damp with the fluid
        of sticky fruit

Two of Pentacles

The crowned serpent
completes the lemniscate.

Blue rings of smoke
blow out the eyes of the bedsheet

ghost. Polliwogs
of light & dark twist in

an authoring conflagration.
New to full, old

to new. Old & new
like a new crack in the watch

crystal; the air will get through
to the hands

at last. More change
falling from the holy pockets

like a tiny tinkling glockenspiel
in a dead poet's parlor.

THREE OF SWORDS

Spikes in the heart
of the white rose
in the hen of the woods, the woods
dumb with garish
humidity. Bats' wings
cleave the summer night,
an overripe fruit
bleeding sweet
on the forest floor.

This is home; I creep
silent along the loam,
peer out from blank black
spaces among the dark
trees, my face wet
with what might have begun
as tears.

BLAST BEAT

Cumulus bank,
an avalanche, advances;
seafoam spit,
a comet disintegrates
in the breath
of death. Cicada music
perforates the summer; a cold
front breaks across the pricks of buildings;
   the seventeen-year sleep
     falls on the thirteenth,
  atonement
  an autumn
     green eyes the
     green wings
     my red hair of winterlong
night. Lovely cirrus interrupt the staff of the power
lines.
     Every year
  I bleed out
noxious equinox,
    not my harvest,
    not my death cult.
  I watched a dead sparrow
  melt into the flagstones
  all August, the hollow katydids
dusty maracas.
    The Puritan winter
  laughs
  in the crossbeams
of the old house.
Always in twilight,
the sound of a bell, bright,
  bringing fever
to the table. The port city wars
   with the ocean; the thunderbirds
bask & rip
up your official documents,
  flowers of ashes
in the hurricane winds.
  Let the jellies rule the seas,
the land anarchic, resplendent with ferns.
  Nobody's home.

WEIRD SISTER

Timeloose agony
built a hive in nostalgia
That stream that
runs uphill
the runnels of which
are varicose
veins, blue as the dark
All those masts
attached to nothing
Bad thoughts
surf the leylines
upside-down kites
Free me, witch
Those pinkest
eyes. Do you recall
those eyes
at all? Stalk
charms curl in
the fire, fingernail
parings alight in deep-
mind, little moons
under the big moon of little
sleep, fleeing the little
death, a long life
cut deep
in the palm. The ruby
vein beneath
the ice. My own
devices scour
the blast crater
for a sign of life
The sign says
Silence please
Can you read me
the signs, sister
witch? Is any
association really
free? A dark house
on a dark road
to say nothing
of the disembodied
eye-lights among
the dust bunnies

who fear not the broom
housekeeping being
antithetical
to magic, which is
the stain of being
on the sallow
cloth of matter
Your shadow
will follow you
until you are just
dust, then it will
join the general
darkness of the void
Good witch
who has eaten her
penumbra, rip me
from myself, make me
a black swan on the black
water, the sea
of stars, the eye
of the storm of
is

NUTS

Pomegranate, poppy seeds
nails in my teeth.
A nut for each age
of a man—a boy's
cyanide almonds,
cashews curved as sex, filberts
brown as shit, impenetrable as Saturn's
return.

I am the walnut
now, bitter brain
in its skull, a boat
for a young mouse. Over the Styx
& through the woods
with sticky butternuts
shook down like laughter, hairy eggs
or tears, to the house
on Black Sabbath's eponymous first
record, the elusive macadamia
on the table,
a mortar & pestle, an epistle
& a stamen, a trumpet
for the days' end, heaven
a grim *ex libris*.
   What is an old man
   drunk on Lucifer's light?
The last dance.
The acorn, the hickory, cheek-pouches
swollen like grenades; the snow
starts; scratch
at the frozen turf, debris ejected
betwixt your crouching legs
& out onto the noonday street, interrupting
the progress of the peanut
seller's cart.

CORONA RADIATA

The pain of the singularity
        cannot be copied,
                analog agony
a stand-alone complex.

Night sweats the superalloy;
        my emblem will be
the hard light that falls
        on the penitent head hung,
heraldry of this embodied grief
        sheathed in chrysoprase
& brass, same as it ever was—
        the wind carries with it
piano music, memories
        of sex, a bar in the East
Village now gone, ruddy leaves
        like the unnamed
city bodies. Where are they now?

Halloween is cancelled;
Halloween is every day
inside this mission to Mars
that never got off
the ground; call it hypersleep,
        call it one summer
that never began.
        When the doors open,
where will we be?
        Prague Spring
for everyone
        except all of the folks
at home;
        Canada geese dart
overhead, not quite a V
        in the pencil dust
sky, looking down they don't
        wonder where
we've gone.

UNITED STATES OF AUTUMN

The dying trees
emit warm
colors, perhaps mistaken
for flowers from the air;
the empire
shakes
like a dancer
in its throes, its colors
       bright & vast,
resplendent wrapped around
       its rotting heart.
No peace
until the fiend sleeps
for the winter
       under bone tines
of waiting trees,
       grey sinews,
dried bees,
       fifty fires
licking at the nests. Taken
to wind, what lived
within: the state bird
mock combat mascot
headed for higher ground—
       the falling bridge,
the bent, shrieking rails: a shroud
of rusty nails on broken
children, a charred tribe
in the charnel
festooned with jewels
       in their mouths
& openings, at each other's throats
for big bright coins
       for their eyes.

PUT YOUR RAYGUN TO MY HEAD

September is the name
of the golem of
crumbling rebar; its xylophone teeth
crack down on our tender
skulls like
an insecticide. Surrender

the crickets of August
under the Rorschach whirligigs
of the maple seeds screwing to earth.
I see an inverted smile;
I see dimetrodon sails;
I see fucking crazy
teaching English
in a town with no umbrellas.

It rains on me & it
rains. My father left me
an adding machine
& a heap of coins
from places we'd never been.

All the things that weren't
my fault had a war
with the things that were
& only a poem survived—
but not this one.

He spent the rest of his life
yelling though a painted-on
crack in the door,
as beautiful as
the worms in the Western Wall
eating prayers

they can't read.

EIGHT OF CUPS

The nectar of storms
& the blood of
the lotus runs
over the murky sea
pocked with green
leaf-forms. The rhizome
floats below flotsam
of brass, adrift
in these still waters
in the green rain
light.

Reading the script of the rain
on the rim of the chalice,
the air thick with mist,
the coast thick with leaves, nowhere
to land so sink down
with the kelp so gently
swaying like someone's hair.

RIVER OF THE MOUNTAIN PLACE

Here comes the pageant of dead leaves
floating on the black water of the river;
watch them twine like a braid of spit
from the eelmouth of October & observe
exhibit ß, the shriveled hand of our lord
spinning weightlessly among
the grimy habits of the penitent,
& here a torn shard of a wall
that abuts a dreadful restaurant
where a man waits to be cast out
to return to the grimy hovel
where his bones are buried; following
closely behind—a fine sylph in a bottle
of Vitamin Water: blueberry
pomegranate açai, the pneumatic slurp
of her song calling the mangy
gulls to the banks where they all
but drown out the farting blat
of the old tugboat as it drags
its net along the bed, stirring the dun silt
in camouflage clouds, obscuring, briefly,
your view from where the jerky
stick of your leg is anchored
to the great schist effigy of Hestia.
The flotsam above, which may
as well be clouds, makes shapes
& shapes, dragging its plague doctor
proboscis among the pocked trees of
chrome & chicken bone where
the filthy American shad dance & now,
high above, the page of this poem itself, torn
loose from its raincoat pocket full of rusted
pennies & liquor store receipts in the mad
dash to the morning train, now a ghost
of its former self, just beyond
your frantic grasp as it rolls,
a twisted origami albatross
on the roof of the river—beetle-skinned
by sapphire bruises of grease
& oil—making its weary way
to the salt sea where a great storm
is churning, turning its blind eye
to observe you there, dancing

to some music that only you
& the carrion crabs can hear.

KNIGHT OF WANDS

for Joanna C. Valente

They ride the black
unicorn with a horn
of flame, reach out for a red
right hand emblazoned
on cinder-blocks beside
the train tracks,
from which gushes ivy
& a great green coal-
hearted aster   smoldering
to diamonds.

They carry a torch & sing
a torch song outside
the tower of blood.
Shoes of iron tap a breakbeat
on the desiccated turf,
the pulse of a dragonfly
tumbling toward burning earth, sky
& flames making a mandala
of gold & grey.

NEPENTHE & GRENADINE

Carry on, eukaryote,
Man is the bastard this time;
Redo everything in enamel
Model paint. No wall
Between living & dying
On Facebook—filling up
With mourners
& finger-food
As in the funeral house.
I have seen nothing
To recommend autumn,
Can barely abide the winter
Sun the color of snow,
The wings of horses,
Not the color of dresses
In stained glass this season,
Marbleized & butter-yellow
Slanting down to the little pine
Table, a slide with flecks
Of glitter dust in suspension
Like the silver pinpricks
In the car paint, causing
Spirit orbs in the orgasm
Of the LED flash; the little pine table
Where you are alone
With the poet, out of sight
Of anyone. Forget about
The tourists, the family,
The meal on the silver dais,
So mealy & pale
While the squirts of slush
Slide down the fogged panes,
The debris of a million ohs
In the crypt of the apartment
Where the real dust rides
A phonograph needle
In the Jack-the-Ripper gloom.

Congratulations.
You're a rider on the afternoon bus,
Not what anyone imagined
Or anyone wants to be,
Whoever they are, their arms full

Of xmas presents, virgin
Plastic pressed up like breasts
In their faces on the escalator.
So good, the lightning lighting up
The front of the restaurant.
A good table, a good catch, the chanteuse
In a gleamy frock mouthing nothing
You can even relate to—
No tragedy, no election, no
Faceless reprobate alums
Out on the squash court, brutal
& clean or in the vein
Of the old new road, a marvel
Of civic engineering for planes,
Steering wheel in the delta
Of parted knees, applauding
Vigorously for all the helicopters
Painting the night
With their bright, downcast eyes.

MELLO YELLO ZERO

It was as though
a face in ice; the heat
of the pizza dissipates
in the noon cold.
There are always other
reasons. You fell
in a poem on the way
there; it was lonely.
You were a cartoon
drunk drinking from
a XXXed bottle.
You were not excited
by the particular
arrangement of trees
or flowers, the body
always wanting
something just like
a baby. Maybe
there were others
or maybe just mirrors;
mothers be kind
to other mothers
& their bad kids
down by the railroad
tracks. You must
pay the rent; you
can't pray for anything
when there's nothing
to pray to or on.
Without ceremony,
but perhaps with
a candy bar or some sort
of novel that doesn't
hurt like the dentist
doesn't hurt. Leave
it there, someone else
will need it. A helping
hand plucks you out
of the poem. There is
no arm attached
to it, only night
sky, only embers.

PHANTOM DESTROYER

As the year begins
in death so do I

Whatever lies
dormant, whatever
waits, dreams

The black that lays bare
errant hairs
& sloughed skin

Negation's
liberation, empty

space the palette
of matter

What dwells in what
is not, a caricature
of bones

A hive of sounds
A face
changes to face
the river

of particles, the classification
& reorganization that is
space, civilization

is buildings, which are
delineated
emptiness

Speak not
of what is,
rather what
cannot is
what must be told;
thus what is not
is what begins
in what is

What lives in never
abounds—
what is desire
is what lies
apart &

within
the sweep
of the eye
& never
the I
of possibility

Mountain of Mirrors

The white dragon
was a brain zap
in high summer,

a mirror of ice
unmelted by the heat.
You didn't choose

your own adventure
so much as one of several
forking paths that led

to a couple of different endings
at most. Your body
began to defect

in the living rooms
of comfortable homes,
the potential normal

you kitten-nape-lifted
by the vicious beak
of that pale serpent & placed

in a crystal palace
with a bunch of similar
souls, never to return

but forced to watch
yourself failing algebra,
jerking off

to the Club MTV dancers
writhing to "Straight Up"
on the night of the prom,

walking out into the heavy rain
& just standing there, staring
back into the empty house.

ACE OF WANDS

In flames
the script
of breath
& death t
he negati
on of dar
kness tha
t harbors
potential
ity; eatin
g away t
he bier, c
hanging
the cold
but for a
moment
only, the
dream o
nly of su
n on fles
h, the da
wn impr
isoned in
a rood, v
ain arbit
er of nig
ht. Flora
of pande
monium,
destroye
r & heart
h-friend,
never sti
ll, but st
ill burni
ng in the
desert &
the noon
like the r
evenant o
f midnig
ht.

VALENTINE

Upon the light that rises
from the snow be gorged—
        the white that sits upon
        the tire-piles with the quickness
of halt. The storm's wherewithal to quell
the rabid popping of the supercollider
        of commerce breaking the spines
        of the particular.
The trees rise up to it;
it is their habit of sleep, the dreams
        of living wood the agency
        of the time of magic, each
abstracted form tucked in like an organ
in the magic body. A spell
        for February,
        for a city can die of lack of love,
for or among her. The people must leave
their homes, but they cannot.
        Listen to the slope-roofed thunder of snow.
        Listen to the claws of birds scrabbling
upon stilled machines. The beat
of melting icicles on a plastic box
        of empty plastic boxes, a vortex hides the traces
        of our useless fidgeting.
The flakes settle in the obliteration of the om,
the gusts of the blood,
        which does not behave like water,
        which rusts the color of low flame—
red is our dream in the sleep of the leaves;
red the inside of our mouths;
        red of the snowbound fox-caught vole,
        red on white the piping
on the dollar-store hearts, the piping of the breath
of a nameless man lost in the erased winter streets.

FOUR OF WANDS

Chaos star tilts & occludes
the velvet sun   partitioned
& blooming
                    ram & dove
are spokes that spin the wheel
that propels the plow
along the sward   The blue eye
of Venus takes heed   All parties
blur in revolution

THE HANGED MAN

A black cross
or a sword; I see
with the eyes
of nails. The coiled cobra
of the horizon is home.
The dark roads lead
to the shrinking point,
the black, collapsing
star over the still waters
where I will be
taken. The ghost sun
will shine on all
the hidden bones
under the skin of things—
crinolines for the funerary
gown. Reverse
the flow of gravity,
see the sky as it is,
an angry sea, be
lowered to the frozen
earth, a secret number,
a casualty.

IT COMES ON YELLOW
after Su Tung P'o

It comes on yellow &
it comes on blue.
It comes for the shapely flowers
& it comes for you.

In the dawn & the gloaming
the shadows climb up & down
the walls, the ceiling blisters
& falls like a snipped bud.

Will you be caught in the net
of barren twig silhouettes
black against the blushing quartz
of the sky? The sky

isn't real & neither are you.
Tend to the garden of your flesh,
how it resists
blight & pestilence, but never

enough. Starlings devour each other
on the curb, transubstantiation
juju for the down-&-out set.
Don't say life is short,

because it is. *How many Spring Festivals are we*
born to see? How many lives led?
In even this one husk?
Youth is a curse on the old,

the magnolias so frail
under the casters of the U.S. Mail—
a new career in the Dead Letter
Office—"Must have a sense of humor

about every goddamned thing."
It comes on red &
it comes on green; it's everything
you've even been, everything you've ever seen.

MY OTHER CAR IS A WILHELM SCREAM

The clouds fight a war
with time & the clouds
always win.

I want to live inside
how someone must have felt
listening to "Heart of Glass"
on the BQE in summer of 1979.

Men with bad breath
know what's good in poetry;
I'm a failure
at being a failure & the world
is full of stupid people.

I grew a mustache
so I wouldn't see my father
in the mirror.

Hair's getting longer;
dandelions fade
to skeletons & then puff away
but they still have shadows.

When you see a plane high
in the sky, remember
there are people inside,
no bigger than the heads of pins.

This poem has no empathy
& isn't relatable.

ATTACK OF THE GIANT ANTS

Among the teeming people,
cowering under the silver star
            of death,
after the icepick
            hammered on the blue
moon; in the habit of poetry, ghoulish
with mothholes, just one drop
            of falling water
is never rain.
                        O moon
you are always the same,
            not like the forces of time
who act upon Debbie Harry,
            the realization
that things were OK for a few weeks
in New York City in the '70s
            but you were too busy
being five years old. O who
will love my corpulent soul
            when I have slain every living thing
with the blade
of August; who will teach the child
math?
            Only the beautiful
things change, an analog
            to digital signal like the waking
from the gauze of sleep
to the real room, as it is,
a singularity. Eaten away
until even the perceiver begins
to change; the purple water
ever at the edges
of the known world, always waiting,
a song in the background:
            La la, la la la, la la, la la la, la la, la la la
            Lost forever,
the last summer of a certain species,
you,
            while the television never creeps
to static anymore,
            the television itself
may go on forever.

42

THE DEVIL

Looping horns akimbo, high
as a gloaming bat above

the avenue where the roots
of trees push up flagstones

like the lids of coffins, outside
of time:

within the lit windows is what happens
in secret—reverse

mitosis; the ascending spirits
pluck the harp of the spindle:

night & day conjoined
in the mystery of their

origin. Indigo stains are the braille
of foxglove's open-

throated hymns as the one sun
is ringed by melancholia—

godhead rides the trap groove
spinning around

the ruby of the third eye.
                    A hoof steps quiet upon the black

ice & radiates a crackling bloom
of unrealized timelines,   walks

soundlessly across the expanse
of frozen mirror upon mirror upon

mirror, communicating
as braided wire or the warzone

of the splitting allele. All shall be
well & all manner

of things shall be undertaken

under the full stop

of the unjoined caduceus.
Open thy arms

& receive

MAYDAY

Fading flag between two April trees
waking from winter, crowded with new
growth; a flag can only tatter & fall
as spring, summer, winter & autumn crash
at boots & buildings as waves. Two worlds—
one vast & old & fomenting, one new & sick
with human things, human lands, rabid
with hunger, with amnesia, who
can do nothing but beat its children down, screaming
for what was once beautiful while withered
plants & animals swarm from the heartlands,
the headlands, the foothills—every orifice
of the land stuffed with radioactive piles,
lousy with oligarchs swollen with heads & bristling
with vestigial cocks as their minions prop them up
with transparent shields & clubs & anything
that can be grasped & swung like a clock hand
going back & forth in a wedge, time clotted
& stuck, iced up & jammed with bodies & garbage,
bodies of garbage, tethered & shackled bodies
in an awful line proceeding up a hill growing
ever higher from their own fallen kin
toward nothing at all—a precipice made of the dead
& diseased & the avaricious ones hiding amongst,
faces smeared with blood, feeling your pain
like the sun feels the moon.

No avatar to lift aloft the conflagration
of the little rage flames, which are love,
the little nightmares, which are memories—
animal memories in human heads, arms
aching to be wings, paws, claws, hooves,
levers & thunderstorms—to cast a stone into the air
that would be a new round world,
that would be a seed planted
firmly in the ground that will swallow the felled
demagogue.

45

FIVE OF PENTACLES

Cracked star over
The stoked furnace.

Pyramid: an offering to
The cruel sky.

Cube: cage of lightning &
The key of lack.

Sphere: but a stage of
Grief, conductor of elegies.

Horns of the moon: the call of
The entombed god.

Black lozenge: the bitter pill
What resolves.

The wounded wheel is a cog in
A clockwork tragedy.

Tears behind the mask &
Tears in the solemn shroud upon

The proscenium, shattered coins for
The bedight throng.

BLAST BEAT

for Lissa Rivera

She was told
the pillars would fall,
as she walked backwards
through the gates, but
the candle flames sprung
from her fingertips & those
flames stung.
She saw the backs of the people
advancing, the sweat
on their necks, those parts
of themselves they
could never see; the ashes
clotted to marigolds, capital
letters majestically stood,
but their voices became
quite small—
the ones who were walking
she knew would fall,
the pink sky above them a slab
of meat, the street
dropped like a shot bird
over the edge & down the sheer
face. *O be careful*
she said as they shrank
into Renaissance perspective & their hats
flew free
from their tumbling heads.

QUEEN OF SPELLS
for Amabel Lamoureux

My body
cannot sustain you
O my daughter

I am just
a bone-mat

All my wit
& all of my art
in abeyance
that you may
land softly
on the altar
of my ribcage

Let Abraham's knife
be broken

I will slay god
for you
& drop him
from my teeth
at your feet

SHAVASANA
for Lori Bonazzoli

The day is glass

Hubris of named hours

A mantra powerful as a plant

What if the dead could vote?

The mighty limbs

The black nerves of the earth

Frame an isthmus of static

Blue & nostalgia the language of sundogs

Pools purple sugar

Water & the insect limbs of sweat

Discomfit a crown of daisies

A ring of poppies a corpse in the sun

Ringing. Silver slash of meteors

& pulverized diamonds

Dip of a beak, a proboscis

Into the moonstone vein

The clear eyes of fireflies

A fire in the dawn heat

A heart

The herm of a second

PRINCE OF CUPS

It's true I rode a green bird
into the ocean in the rain
next to the amusement park
& its haloed lights, grey
whorls of clouds reflected
in the indolent surf.

The wheels of my emerald car
dug grooves in the sand
& my winding path
in the shape of the Oroborous
snake could be seen
from the air, along with the fallen
petals of the bouquet I
clutched & at last threw
into the sea.

Willow, weep for me;
I lay down beneath the willow tree,
its limbs bent like wings,
went to sleep forever
& woke something new.

THE FOOL

At the center of the gnomon
the Green Man wakes & sleeps, angel
with butterfly wings
twisting the rainbow
in a lover's knot
while the infernal beasts
lie at her feet. God
of the grain rounds the four
corners of the circle of death
& life seeps out the hole
in his blasted head, eyes
red with the fruit of the vine.

A dove alights on a burning bush
in the ruins of Thebes, a severed
head begins to sing of the time
before birth as the sun sets
in the west. She tears a hole
in the firmament & laughs
in at himself. The white rose
eclipses the moon & the new day
begins to end.

Song for Noa Pothoven

& a clear bell rings
at the end of all things;

every ash, every ember flits
home, grey birds of annihilation;

the wine-dark of oblivion
swells, a wave that only crests

& whorls of darkness, dolphins
surfing the ripple of unmaking,

crashing in a kind of joy
through the veil of being

& stumbling to rise, fawn-legged
& new in the perfect,

still point of nothingness
where pain is the same as green leaves

or dwarf stars. The night-winged
devas lift high the wordless

banners & the smallest cry
will amplify & pulverize

worlds like pills. Everything
which once was now smaller

than the hole in every letter
of every word,

every powerless word—
the sin of matter

now avenged.
Let it all be gone & let

the ghost of it
be gone too.

HYMN TO OIZYS

My body is
        the prayer

A dead star
        is the answer

There is a place
        blacker than the night

There is a flame
        colder than the void

There is a hunger
        stronger than love

There is a face
        in the ashes of the offerings

It is my own

What is taken
        is never given

You will take
        what is yours

You will take
        everything

& not want
        & not see

& not love
        & not exult

In the corporeal
        collapsing

Into the hole
        of your heart

You never asked
to be born

You need not
        ask

To die

Because the answer
        is exploding space

The words
        that fall apart

As soon as they are spoken

The poem
        that cannot end

But must end
        in you

AFTERWORD: GLYPH FOR THE TURNING YEAR

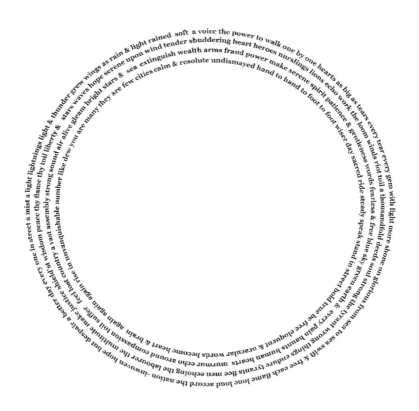

NOTES

Frimaire: Frimaire was the third month in the French Revolutionary Calendar (November 20 – December 21). This book begins & ends in December.

Misericordate: A misericorde was a small stiletto used to deal the death-blow to an armored knight by piercing the unarmored armpit, into the heart, or through the eye-holes of the helmet, into the brain.

Mekoche: Among the Shawnee Indians, the Mekoche were the division of the tribe associated with food and healing. This poem is an appeal to them.

Song for Beth Harmon Who Doesn't Exist: Beth Harmon is the name of the protagonist of Walter Tevis' novel Queen's Gambit & the Netflix miniseries of the same name.

The Helm of Sorrow: Title comes from the song of the same name by Emma Ruth Rundle & Thou. Tanelorn is a city in Michael Moorcock's Eternal Champion mythos.

Weird Sister: "Timeloose" and "deep mind" taken from *Radix* by A.A. Attanasio.

Put Your Raygun to My Head: Title comes from the song "Moonage Daydream" by David Bowie.

River of the Mountain Place: "Housatonic" means "River of the Mountain Place" in Mohican.

Corona Radiata: A stand-alone complex is a phenomenon wherein behavior by unconnected individuals creates a seemingly concerted effort.

Mountain of Mirrors: Title comes from the Dungeons & Dragons Endless Quest book of the same name by Rose Estes, published in 1982.

It Comes on Yellow: Italicized text from the poem "Spring" by Su T'ung Po, translated by Kenneth Rexroth.

Attack of the Giant Ants: Title comes from the song of the same name by Blondie.

Song for Noa Pothoven: Noa Pothoven was a Dutch mental health activist & author who died in 2019.

Hymn to Oizys: Oizys is the Greek goddess of misery, anxiety, grief, depression, and misfortune, daughter of Nyx and Erebus.

Glyph for the Turning Year: In December 2016, just following the shock of the election, I saw a film called "The Arrival" based on a short story by Ted Chiang about the visitation of an enigmatic group of aliens called the Heptapods who show up on Earth for reasons that cannot be determined at the start of the narrative. Attempts to communicate with the aliens reveal that they "speak" by way of inky symbols that they project from their limbs in the form of intricate circular glyphs; each circle is a complete sentence unto itself & must be read all at once & the Heptapods must conceive of the entire content of the sentence before it is generated. So it occurred to me to construct my own Heptapod glyph—the circle is a powerful symbol, conveying steadfast strength & invoking a portal or an open eye or mouth. I wanted to fashion something that would be useful for people & something that might act as a bit of a totem or shield for the times ahead. Since the Heptapod glyphs are conceived all at once, I didn't want to employ the traditional process of writing so I decided I would disassemble an already extant text into the glyph: dissecting something already written would help to dilute my own sense of linearity. I chose Percy Bysshe Shelly's "The Mask of Anarchy" as it, too, was a response to a shocking & pivotal social catastrophe, in this case the Peterloo Massacre of 1819. Shelly's poem, however, was not published until ten years after his death due to the British Government's restrictions of the radical press in the tumult that followed the Massacre. Then I excerpted words from the text & assembled them into a poem of concentric rings that could be read starting at any point & in any direction. To the Heptapods, time is circular & events are perceived simultaneously—in this sense everything is always as it should be in the universe: joys & tribulations are seen in their beginning & their end from a point outside of linear causality. Cause & effect are one. As a conflagration begins we can also see superimposed upon it its end.

ACKNOWLEDGMENTS

"The Devil" appeared in *Yes Poetry*.

"Foolscap," "Mello Yello Zero," and "Mountain of Mirrors" appeared in *spoKe*.

"Foreword: This Machine Kills Fascists" appeared in *Resist Much / Obey Little. Inaugural Poems to the Resistance.* It also appears in the libretto of Ian Wilson's "How Goes the Night?"

"Mekoche" appeared in *Fence*.

"Nepenthe & Grenadine" appeared in *Ping Pong*.

"Valentine" appeared in *FOR ONE BOSTON*.

"Attack of the Giant Ants," "Weird Sister" & "Phantom Destroyer" appeared in *Elderly* magazine.

Thanks to Chris McCreary, Rachel Chatalbash, Kevin Gallagher, Lori Bonazzoli, Basil and Martha King, Kathryn Pringle, Amabel Lamoureux, Andrew Levy, Vivek Narayanan, Lissa Rivera, Maria Teutsch, Ian Wilson, and Joanna Valente.

WHITE STAG